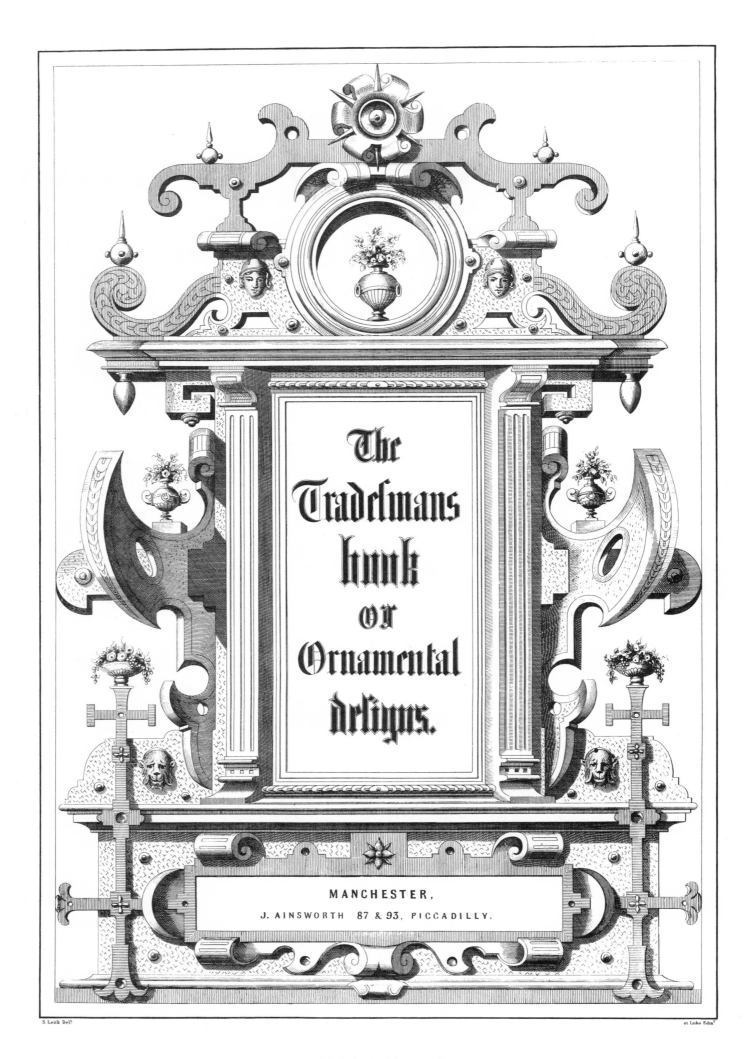

The Tradesmans book or Ornamental designs.

MANCHESTER,
J. AINSWORTH 87 & 93, PICCADILLY.

[Original title page]

Victorian Ornaments and Designs

Samuel Leith

DOVER PUBLICATIONS, INC.
Mineola, New York

Published in Canada by General Publishing Company, Ltd., 30 Lesmill Road, Don Mills, Toronto, Ontario.

Bibliographical Note

This Dover edition, first published in 1999, is a republication of all the plates from *The Tradesman's Book of Ornamental Designs,* as published by J. Ainsworth, Manchester, England, in 1847.

DOVER *Pictorial Archive* SERIES

Library of Congress Cataloging-in-Publication Data

Leith, Samuel.
    Victorian ornaments and designs / Samuel Leith.
       p. cm. — (Dover pictorial archive series)
    "A republication of all the plates from The tradesman's book of ornamental designs, as published by J. Ainsworth, Manchester, England, in 1847."
    ISBN 0-486-40702-0 (pbk.)
    1. Decoration and ornament—Victorian style—Catalogs. I. Title. II. Series.

NK1378 .L45 1999
745.4'4941'09034—dc21
                                                    99-047030

Manufactured in the United States of America
Dover Publications, Inc., 31 East 2nd Street, Mineola, N.Y. 11501

TO THE HONOURABLE

THE BOARD OF TRUSTEES FOR MANUFACTURES

ETC. ETC.

IN SCOTLAND

This Work on

ORNAMENTAL DESIGN

IS BY SPECIAL PERMISSION

DEDICATED

BY THEIR VERY OBEDIENT SERVANT

Samuel Leith

IRON WORK

1

PERFORATED RAIL—EGYPTIAN

3

CARPETING—EGYPTIAN

TRELLIS WORK—GOTHIC

PERFORATED RAIL—GOTHIC

SCROLL &c.—GOTHIC

8   IRON GATE—GRECIAN

PERFORATED RAIL—GRECIAN

DAMASK TABLE COVER—GRECIAN

PATERA—ROMAN

12

14   LAMPS &c.—ROMAN

LAMPS &c.—ROMAN

PERFORATED RAIL—ALHAMBRA

ALHAMBRA—BOOK COVER

PAPER HANGINGS—ARABESQUE

ARABESQUES

ARABESQUES

CEILINGS—ELIZABETHAN

CEILINGS—ELIZABETHAN

23

24   SHIELDS—ELIZABETHAN

SHIELDS—ELIZABETHAN25

26

CEILINGS—ELIZABETHAN

27

28

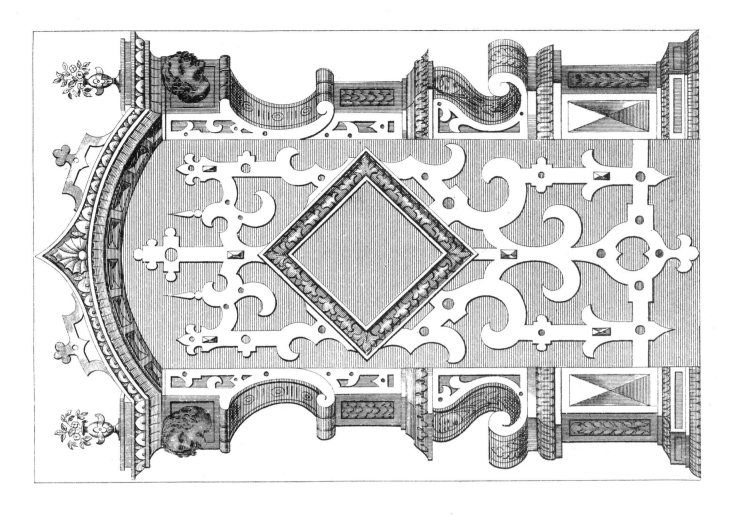

CEILINGS—ELIZABETHAN

30

CEILINGS—ELIZABETHAN

ORNAMENTAL PERFORATED RAIL—ELIZABETHAN

ORNAMENTAL PERFORATED RAIL—ELIZABETHAN

33

34   WINDOW HEADS &c.—ELIZABETHAN

WINDOW HEADS &c.—ELIZABETHAN

GROTESQUE—ITALIAN

From a Rare Etching by Guido Reni after Lucas Cambiaso.

ITALIAN

ORNAMENTAL PERFORATED RAIL—ITALIAN

ORNAMENTAL PERFORATED RAIL—ITALIAN

BORDERS—ITALIAN

BORDERS—ITALIAN

43

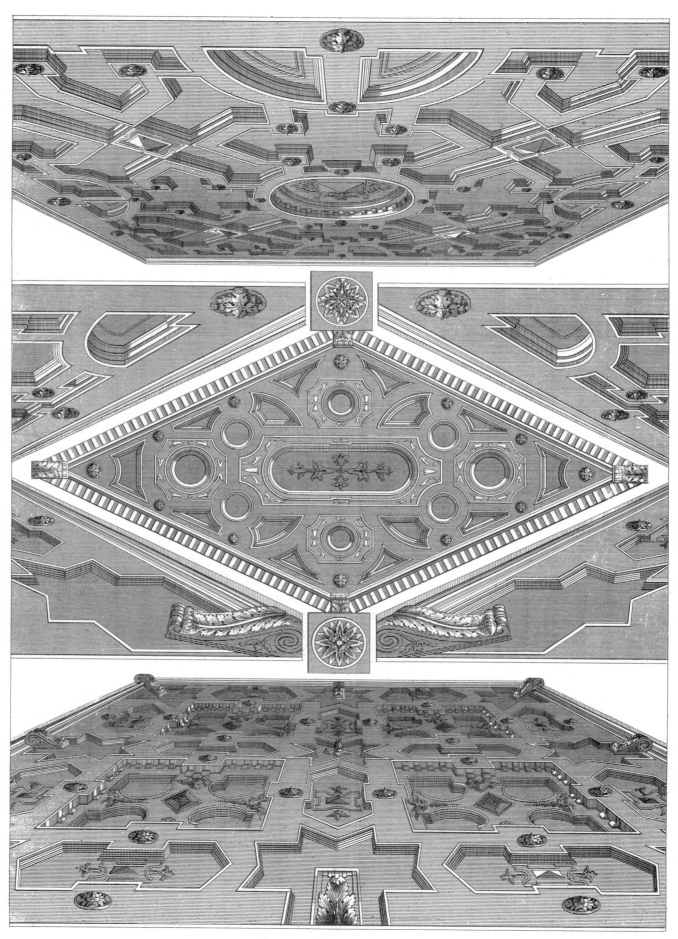

44   CEILINGS—ITALIAN

FIRE SCREEN—GROTESQUE 45

46   TRELLIS WORK—FLEMISH

BOOK COVER—FLEMISH

48   FLEMISH

50

MOORISH AND FLEMISH   51

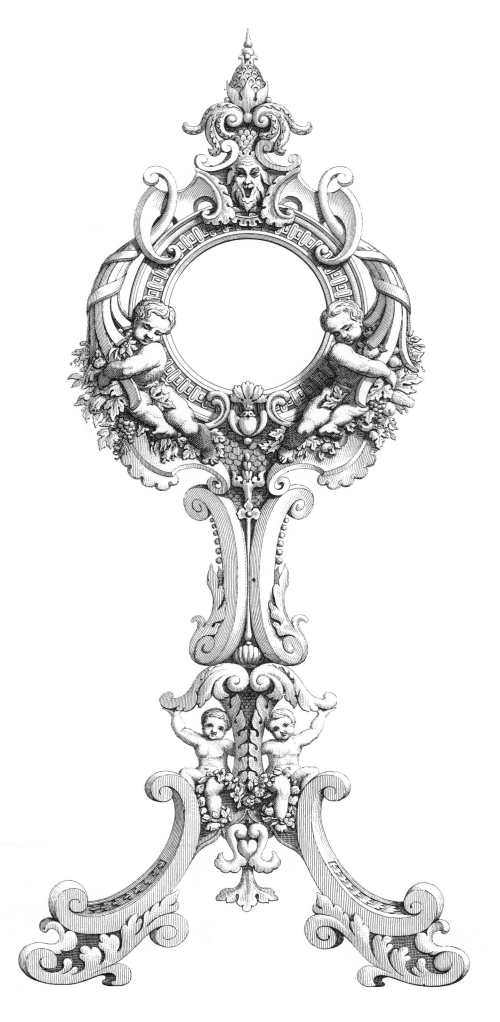

MOORISH AND FLEMISH

LOUIS QUATORZE

LOUIS QUATORZE

INTERIOR DECORATION—FRENCH

1. LOUIS QUATORZE

2. FLEMISH

56

3. MOORISH

4. ARABESQUE

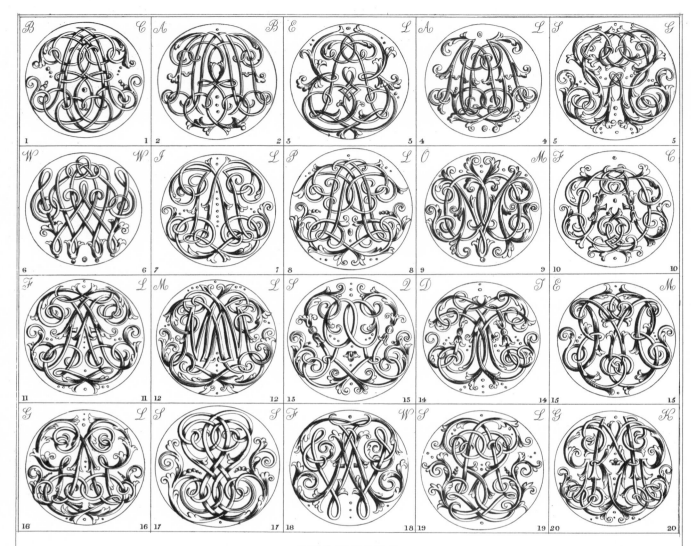

EXAMPLES

for the Ready Composition of any Cypher consisting of 3,4 or more Letters.

Suppose the required letters to be *ABC*, though any others will produce the same effect:

1st Take the two last letters *BC* Cypher *Nº 1*, fold your paper in the middle and draw the one half only of *BC* in plain double lines without Ornament as represented in *Nº 21*.

2nd Add *A* to *BC* already drawn in the same manner as you there find it interwoven with the *B*, Cypher *Nº2*. and as represented in *Nº 22*. then reverse the whole as in *Nº 23* and you will have the entire draught at once.

Fill up the vacant spaces with ornament as in *Nº 24*.

By the foregoing Rules and Examples, Cyphers consisting of *ABCD* or any other Letters may be Composed, by first drawing the two last letters *CD*, to which prefix *B* as in *BC*, and then *A* as in *AB*, shewn in *Nº 25* which reverse as in *Nº 26* and fill up as in *Nº 27*.

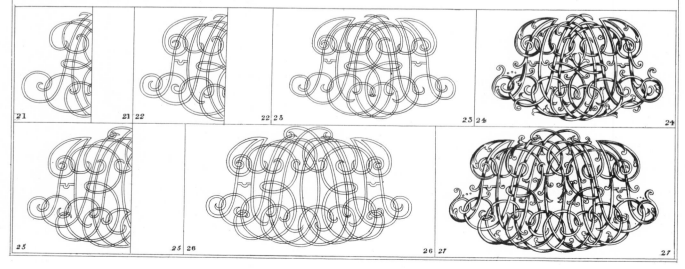